French - Hungarian

LEARNING FLASHCARDS

FOR BABIES TODDLERS

alligator

aligátor

The alligator is having a party.

fourmi

hangya

The ant is red.

ours

medve

The bear loves you.

abeille

méh

The bee is saying hello.

oiseau

madár

The bird is flying.

papillon

pillangó

The butterfly is pretty.

chameau

teve

The camel has a hump.

chat

macska

The cat is happy.

dinosaure

dinoszaurusz

The dinosaur is laying eggs.

poulet

csirke

The chicken is dancing.

vache

tehén

The cow has a bell.

cerf

szarvas

The reindeer has a toy.

chien

kutya

The dog has two floppy ears.

dauphin

delfin

The dolphin is swimming.

canard

kacsa

The duck has a bow.

aigle

sas

The eagle is looking for food.

l'éléphant

elefánt

The elephant is sitting.

poisson

hal

The fish is a clownfish.

libellule

szitakötő

The dragonfly is blue.

renard

róka

The fox has a red nose.

grenouille

béka

The frog is smiling.

girafe

zsiráf

The giraffe has a long neck.

chèvre

kecske

The goat has a beard

ver de terre

féreg

The worm is in the apple

poule

tyúk

The hen has chicks.

hippopotame

víziló

The hippo is big.

cheval

ló

The horse is fast.

kangourou

kenguru

The kangaroo has a baby.

chaton

cica

The kitten is playing.

lion

oroszlán

The lion has a mane.

homard

homár

The lobster is red.

singe

majom

The monkey has a tail.

poulpe

polip

The octopus has food.

hibou

bagoly

The owls have big eyes.

panda

pandamackó

The panda wears a diaper.

porc

malac

The pig is fat and pink.

chiot

kölyökkutya

The dog is brown.

lapin

nyúl

The rabbit has a carrot.

rat

patkány

The mouse is writing something.

crabe

rák

The crab has two pinchers.

requin

cápa

The shark is scary.

mouton

juh

The sheep are very fluffy.

escargot

csiga

The snail is slow.

serpent

kígyó

The snake has poison.

araignée

pók

The spider is purple.

écureuil

mókus

The squirrel has a nut.

tigre

tigris

The tiger has a red bow.

tortue

teknősbéka

The turtle has a shell.

loup

farkas

The wolf is smiling.

zèbre

zebra

The zebra is black and white.

dinde

pulyka

The turkey has two legs.

coq

kakas

The rooster will crow.

perroquet

papagáj

The parrot is colorful.

hérisson

sündisznó

The hedgehog has apples.

pomme

alma

The apple has a leaf.

abricot

sárgabarack

The apricot is yellow.

avocat

avokádó

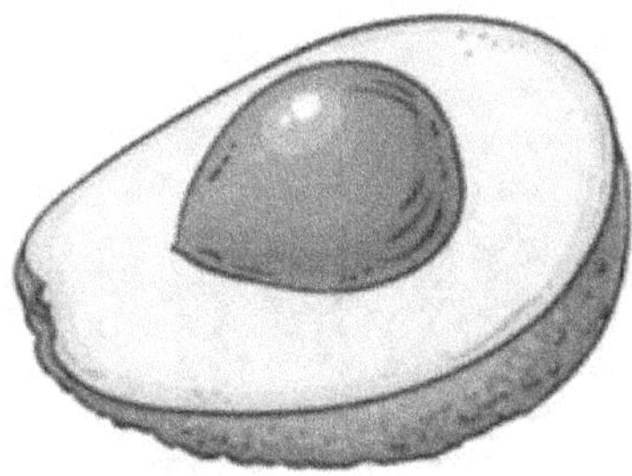

The avocado has a nut.

banane

banán

The banana is yellow.

la mûre

földi szeder

There are a lot of blackberries.

cassis

fekete ribizli

The blackcurrants are yummy.

myrtille

áfonya

The blueberries are sweet.

cerise

cseresznye

The cherries have a stem.

noix de coco

kókuszdió

The coconuts have juice.

figues

füge

The fig has seeds.

grain de raisin

szőlő

The grapes are purple.

pamplemousse

grapefruit

The grapefruits are sour.

kiwi

kiwi

The kiwi is fresh.

citron

citrom

The lemons are yellow.

citron vert

mész

We have lots of lime.

litchi

licsi

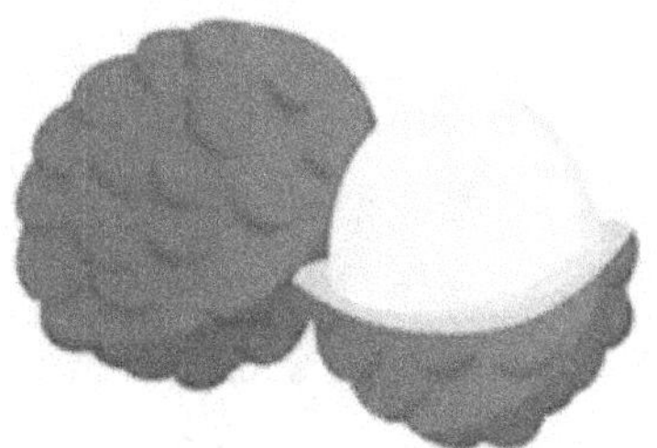

I like to eat lychee.

mandarine

mandarin narancs

Oranges are refreshing.

mangue

mangó

Mango is my favorite fruit.

orange

narancs

Mandarins are like oranges.

papaye

papaya

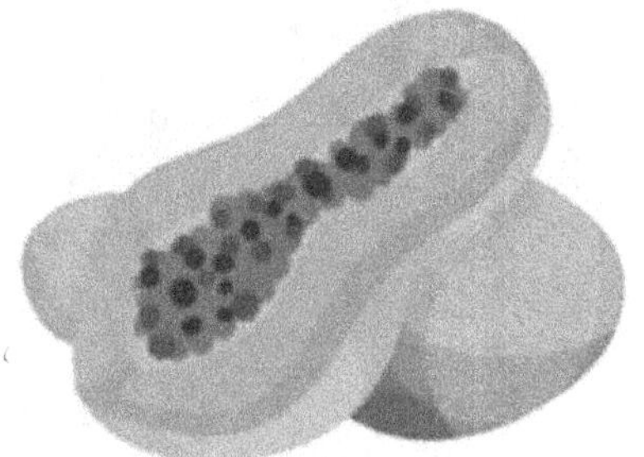

Papayas have lots of seeds.

pêche

őszibarack

Peaches are juicy.

poire

körte

Pears have a strange figure.

ananas

ananász

The pineapple has a thumbs up.

prune

szilva

Plums are healthy for you.

grenade

gránátalma

Pomegranates are all red.

framboise

málna

The raspberry is shiny.

fraise

eper

The strawberry has leaves on top.

pastèque

görögdinnye

The watermelon is big.

mandarine

mandarin

The tangerine looks like an orange.

tarte

pite

I like to eat apple pie.

gâteau

torta

That cake is huge.

bonbons

cukorka

Candy is not good for your teeth.

biscuit

aprósütemény

Cookies are easy to make.

donut

fánk

I like strawberry donuts.

crème glacée

jégkrém

The ice cream is melting.

muffin

muffin

The muffin has a cute wrapper.

pudding

puding

We eat pudding on Christmas.

classeur

kötőanyag

I keep pictures in my binder.

livre

könyv

I like to eat books.

sac à dos

hátizsák

The backpack has lots of stuff.

les ciseaux

olló

I have scissors in my bag.

épingles

pins

Pins can hold stuff up.

agrafe

csipesz

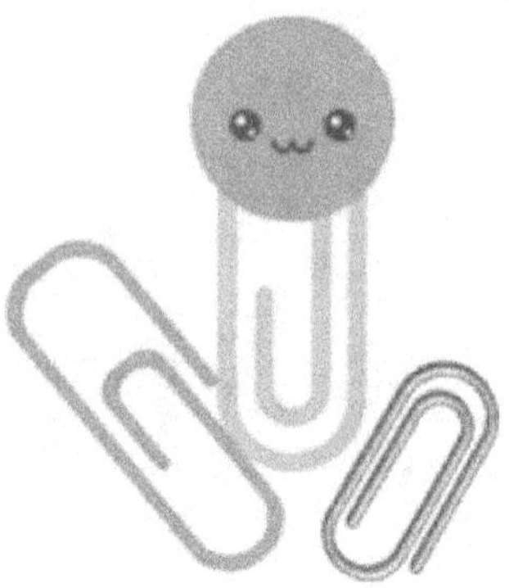

Clips can hold up paper.

papier

papír

I have lots of paper.

agrafeuse

tűzőgép

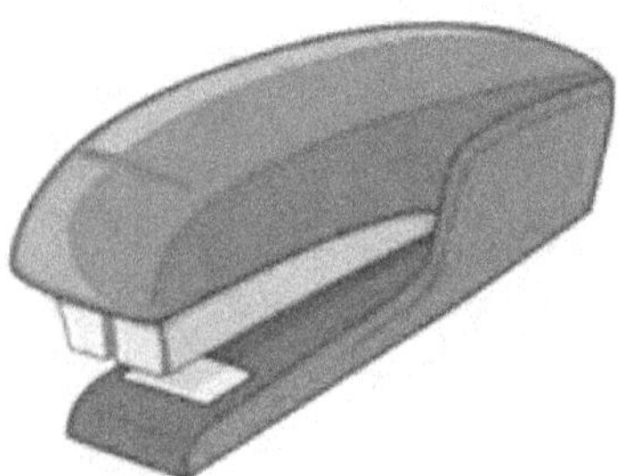

My stapler is shiny and red.

calculatrice

számológép

My calculator has buttons.

règle

vonalzó

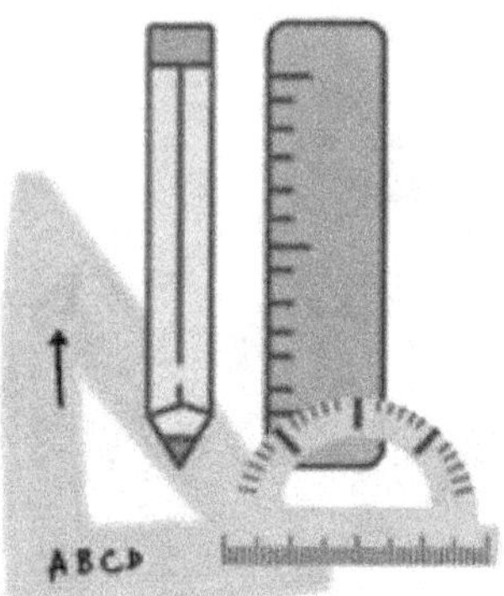

I have lots of rulers.

la colle

ragasztó

The glue is sticky.

bibliothèque

könyvszekrény

My bookcase has lots of things.

calendrier

naptár

I have a calendar on my table.

chaise

szék

My chair is fancy.

l'horloge

óra

The clock says that it's 3 o'clock.

ordinateur

számítógép

I do things on my computer.

bureaux

asztalok

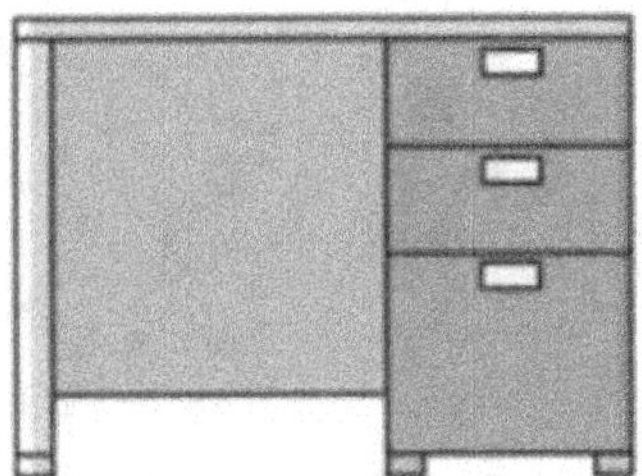

I put lots of things on my desk.

dictionnaire

szótár

The dictionary has lots of words.

la gomme

radír

Erasers are used with pencils.

carte

térkép

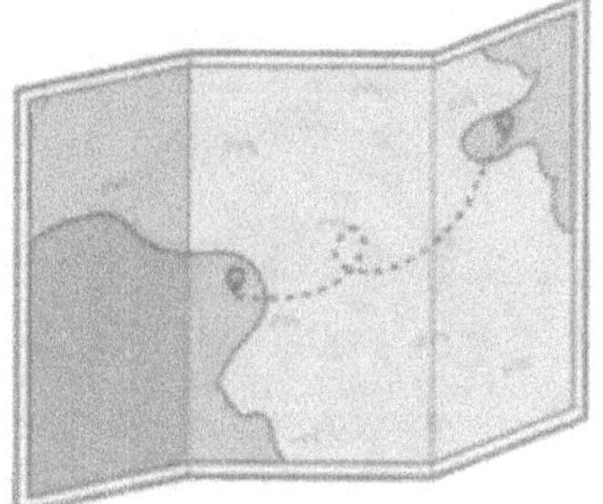

The map shows you different places.

carnet

jegyzetfüzet

I use notebooks at school.

stylo

toll

My pen is very pretty.

crayon

ceruza

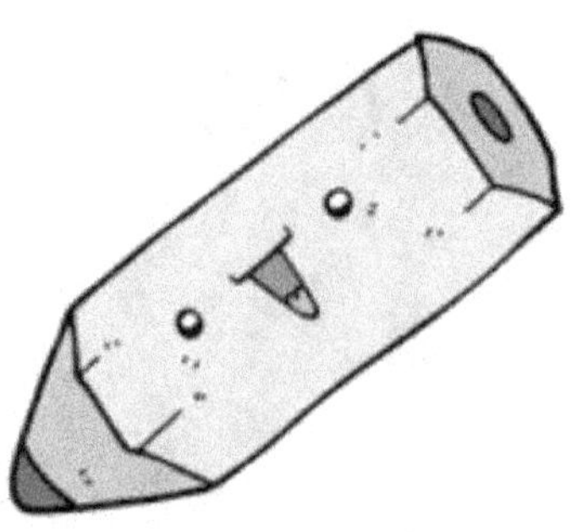

My friend gave me a pencil.

ceinture

öv

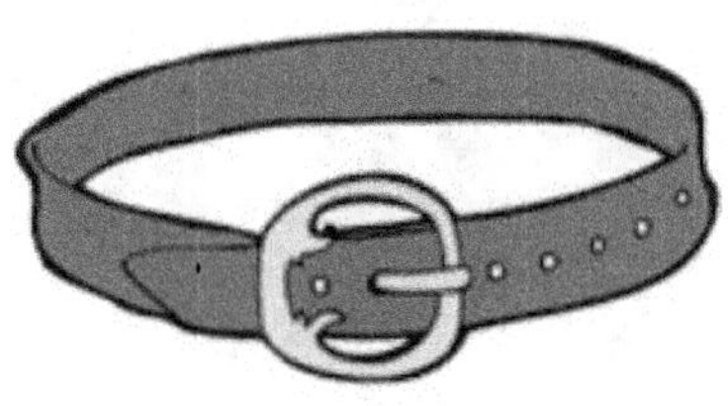

I have a belt on my pants.

bottes

csizma

I have big brown boots.

chapeau

kalap

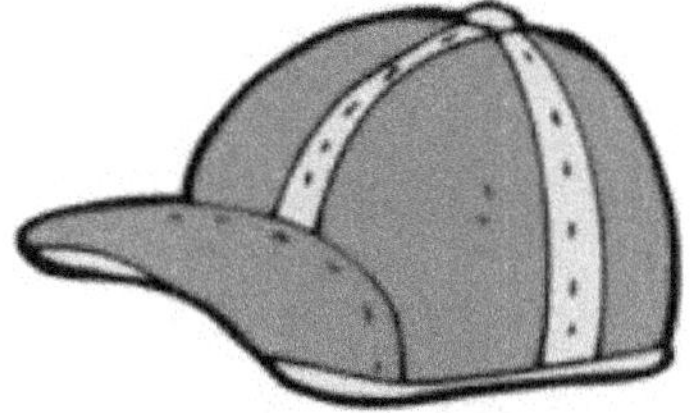

My mom bought me a new cap.

manteau

kabát

She has a long yellow coat.

robes

ruhák

My dress has a bow.

gants

kesztyű

I got new gloves.

chapeau

kalap

That hat is for a wicked witch.

veste

dzseki

The jacket is cozy.

jeans

farmer

My jeans are long.

pyjamas

pizsama

I sleep in my pajamas.

un pantalon

nadrág

The bear is wearing pants.

imperméable

esőkabát

We wear our raincoats when it is raining.

écharpe

sál

The baby has a scarf around his neck.

chemise

ing

I like this shirt the best.

des chaussures

cipő

I have red and blue shoes.

jupe

szoknya

My skirt has lots of buttons.

pantalon

nadrág

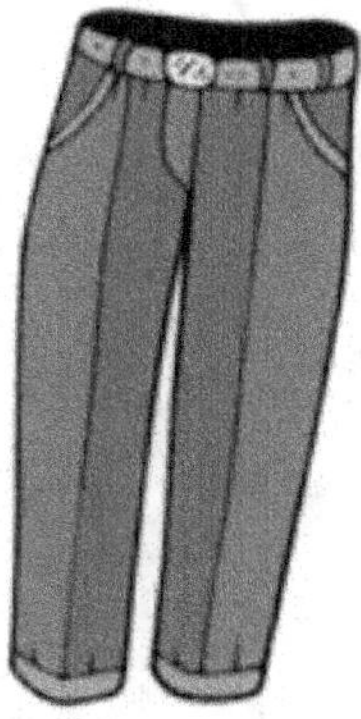

My dad wears slacks.

chaussons

papucs

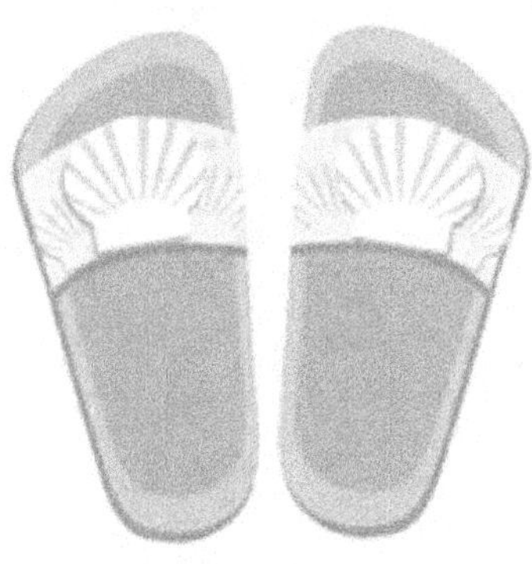

I have seashells on my sandals.

chaussettes

zokni

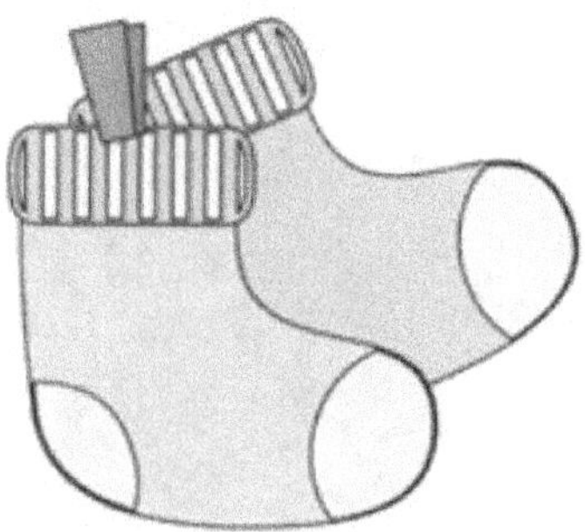

My baby sister wears socks.

costume

öltöny

My brother is wearing a suit.

chandail

pulóver

I am wearing a sweater for winter.

cravate

nyakkendő

My dad wears a tie to meetings.

pantalon

nadrág

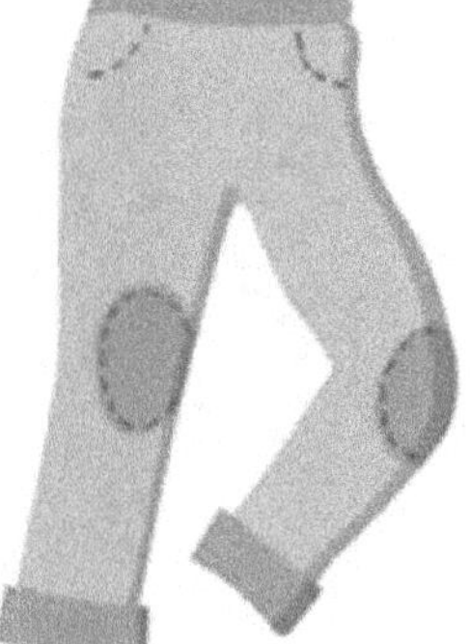

The trousers look like jeans.

slip

alsónadrág

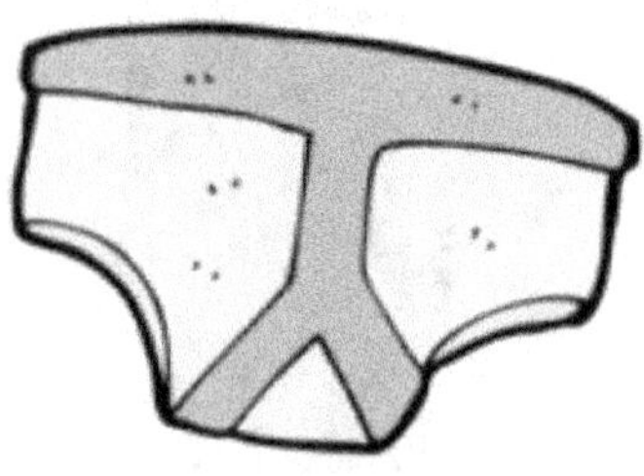

I always wear my underwear.

maillot de corps

trikó

My undershirt has a star.

une

egy

Number one and the bee are friends.

deux

kettő

The cat and the mouse both love two.

trois

három

The bear gives number three a present.

quatre

négy

Number four is a home for the cat.

cinq

öt

Number five hatches an egg.

six
hat

Number six is going to eat a carrot.

sept
hét

Number seven is playing with the tiger.

huit
nyolc

Number eight is funny.

neuf
kilenc

Number nine meets the parrot.

dix
tíz

Number ten is smiling.

onze
tizenegy

Number eleven has big eyes.

douze

tizenkét

Number twelve is number one and two.

treize

tizenhárom

Number thirteen is excited.

quatorze

tizennégy

The number fourteen is vast.

quinze

tizenöt

The number fifteen is green.

seize

tizenhat

Sixteen is my lucky number.

dix-sept

tizenhét

Number seventeen look alike.

dix-huit

tizennyolc

Number eighteen will go to the circus.

dix-neuf

tizenkilenc

I am nineteen now!

vingt

húsz

Number twenty has a zero.

fourmi

hangya

The ant has lots of legs.

cloche

harang

The bell will ring.

vache

tehén

The cow has a bow.

poupée

baba

She has a cute bear doll.

oeuf

tojás

The chick has hatched out of the egg.

poisson

hal

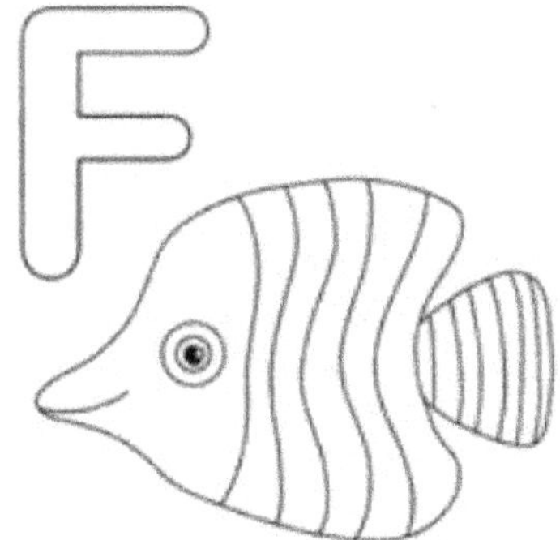

The fish is swimming in the water.

chèvre

kecske

The goat is sitting on the grass.

chapeau

kalap

He is wearing a hat.

crème glacée

jégkrém

I like to eat ice cream.

confiture

lekvár

The kitten is sitting on the jam jar.

chaton

cica

The cat is sleeping on the floor.

lion

oroszlán

The lion is waiting for the tiger.

rat

patkány

The mouse has lots of presents.

nez

orr

The reindeer has a red nose.

hibou

bagoly

The owl is sleeping.

porc

malac

The pig will eat cupcakes.

reine

királynő

The queen has a big crown.

lapin

nyúl

The rabbit is jumping up and down.

mouton

juh

The sheep have fluffy wool.

tortue

teknősbéka

The turtle has a shell.

parapluie

esernyő

The mouse is holding an umbrella.

van

kisteherautó

The van is driving along the road.

pastèque

görögdinnye

The watermelon has lots of seeds.

xylophone

xilofon

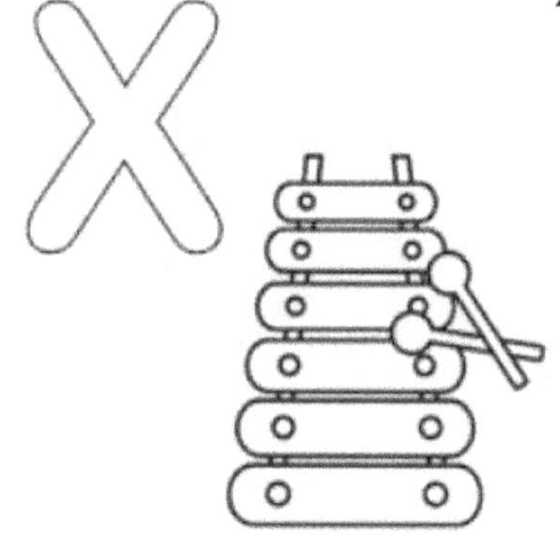

We are going to play the
xylophone.

yaourt

joghurt

We opened the yogurt can.

zèbre

zebra

The zebra is surprised.

rose

rózsaszín

color the word and
the picture in pink

Most of my clothes are pink.

marron

barna

color the word and
the picture in pink

brown

My chocolate is brown.

gris

szürke

color the word and
the picture in pink

gray

I don't like the color gray.

vert

zöld

color the word and
the picture in pink

green

The vegetables are green.

jaune

sárga

color the word and
the picture in pink

yellow

Bananas are yellow.

blanc

fehér

color the word and
the picture in pink

white

The paper that I write on is white.

rouge

piros

color the word and
the picture in pink

red

Apples are red.

bleu

kék

The night sky is blue.

percer

fúró

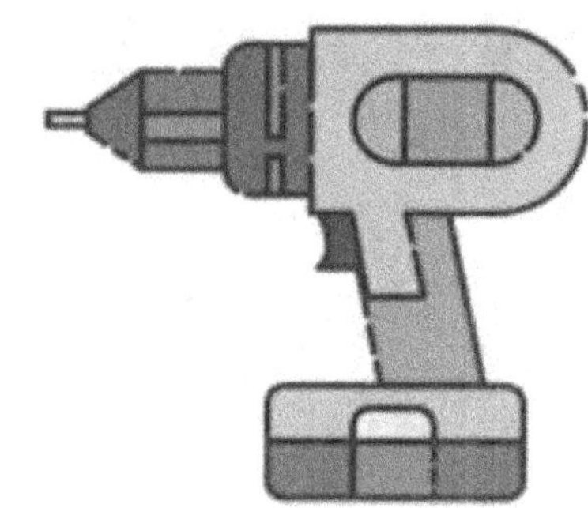

The drill will help us fix this.

marteau

kalapács

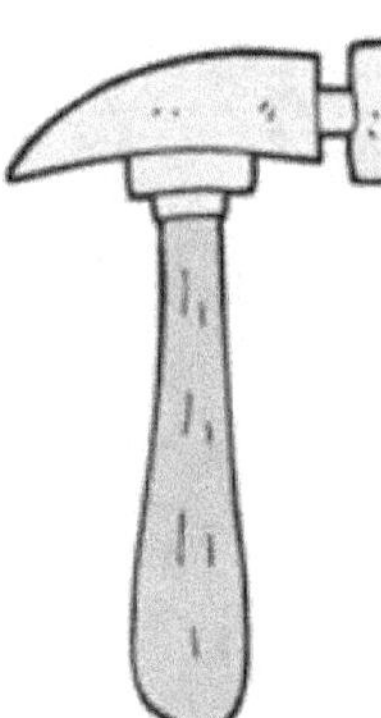

The hammer is going to nail the picture.

couteau

kés

The knife is sharp.

pinces

fogó

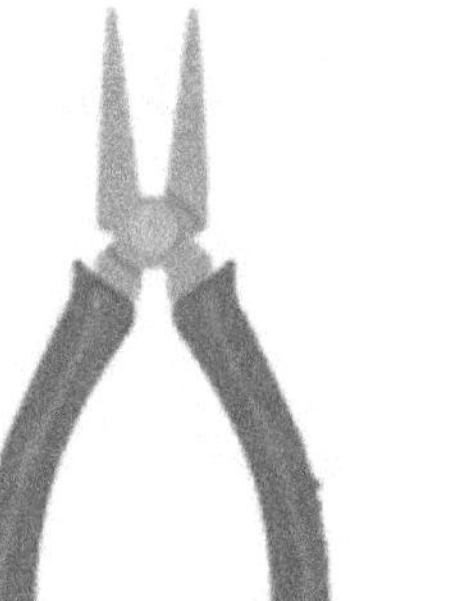

The plier is used for many things.

vu

fűrész

The saw can chop wood.

les ciseaux

olló

I use scissors to cut paper.

tournevis

csavarhúzó

The screwdriver can screw in the knots.

clé

csavarkulcs

The wrench can help unscrew the knots.

avion

repülőgép

The airplane is going to leave now.

vélo

kerékpár

The bicycle is beautiful.

bateau

hajó

The boat is floating on the water.

autobus

busz

The bus is going to school.

voiture

autó

The car is green.

hélicoptère

helikopter

The helicopter is looking for something.

cheval

ló

You can ride the horse.

jet

vadászgép

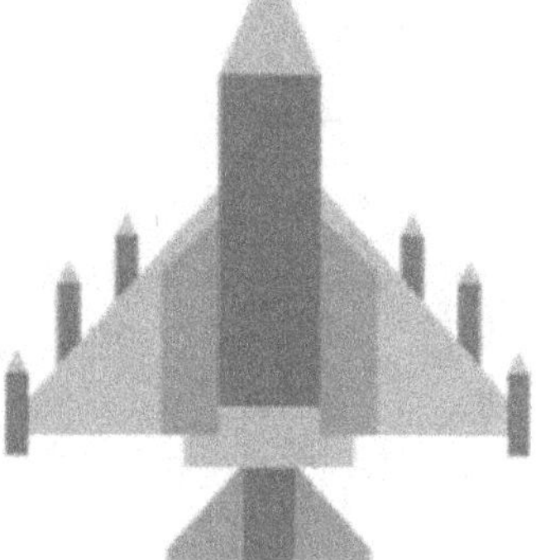

The jet is high-speed.

moto

motorbicikli

The motorcycle is on the road.

navire

hajó

The ship is on the water.

métro

metró

My mom goes on the subway to work.

taxi

taxi

The taxi has someone inside.

train

vonat

The train is going slowly.

un camion

kamion

The truck has stuff in it.

asperges

spárga

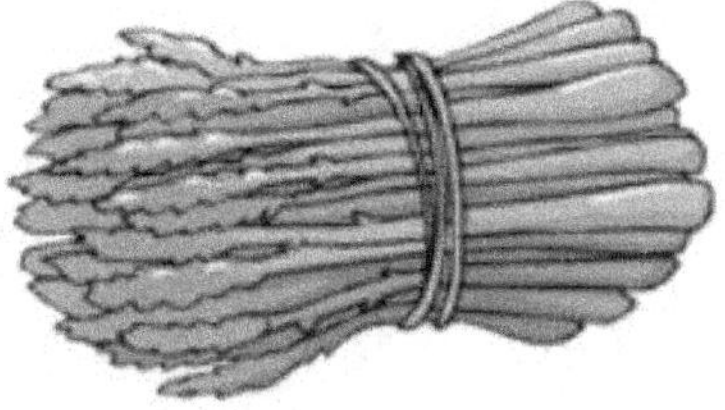

The asparagus is in a bundle.

des haricots

bab

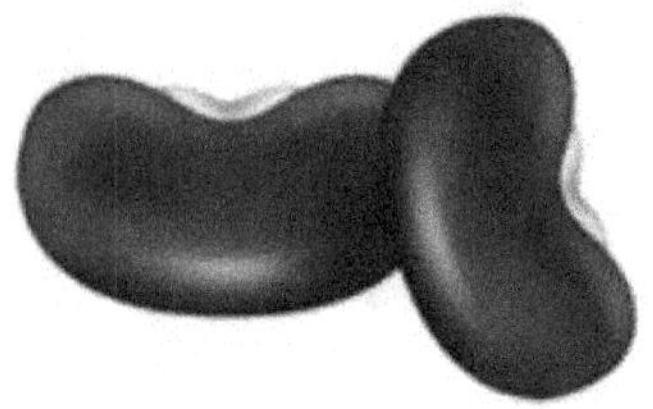

The beans are smooth.

brocoli

brokkoli

The broccoli is dancing.

chou

fejes káposzta

Bunnies like to eat cabbage.

carotte

sárgarépa

The carrots are very long.

céleri

zeller

The celery has lots of leaves.

blé

kukorica

Corn soup is delicious.

concombre

uborka

The cucumbers are cut into pieces.

aubergine

padlizsán

The eggplant is purple.

poivre vert

zöldpaprika

The green pepper is juicy.

salade

saláta

The lettuce is all green.

oignon

hagyma

The onions make my eyes water.

pois

borsó

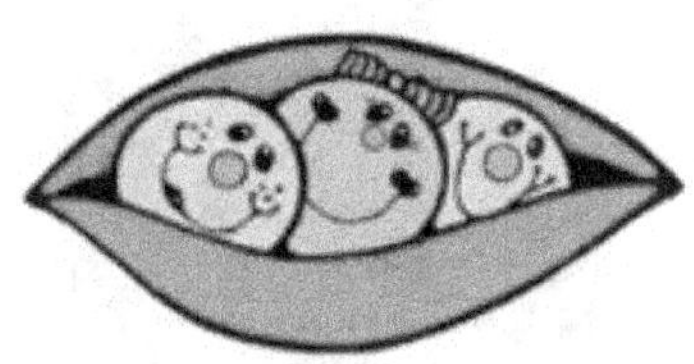

The peas are all in a pod.

patate

burgonya

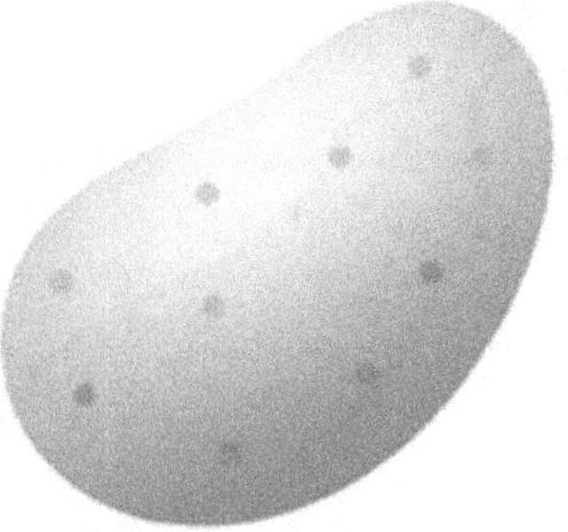

The potato is very shiny.

citrouille

tök

The pumpkin is for Halloween.

un radis

retek

The radish is a type of vegetable.

épinard

spenót

The spinach is good with cheese.

patate douce

édesburgonya

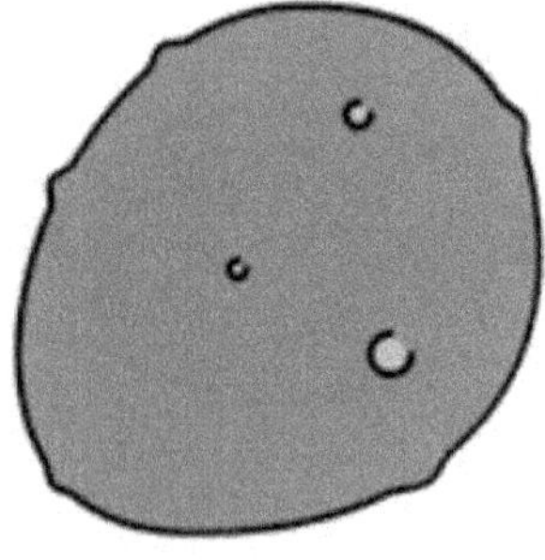

The sweet potato is quite sweet.

tomate

paradicsom

I don't like to eat tomatoes.

navet

fehér retek

My mom bought some turnips.

nuageux

felhős

The weather is cloudy today.

du froid

hideg

I like cold weather.

cool

menő

The temperature is cold today.

brumeux

ködös

The fog is so strong I can't see the city.

chaud

forró

The fire is burning hot.

humide

nedves

It's so humid and wet today.

pluvieux

esős

It's raining very hard.

neigeux

havas

Welcome to snow land!

orageux

viharos

I hate the stormy weather.

ensoleillé

napos

The sun is shining!

chaud

meleg

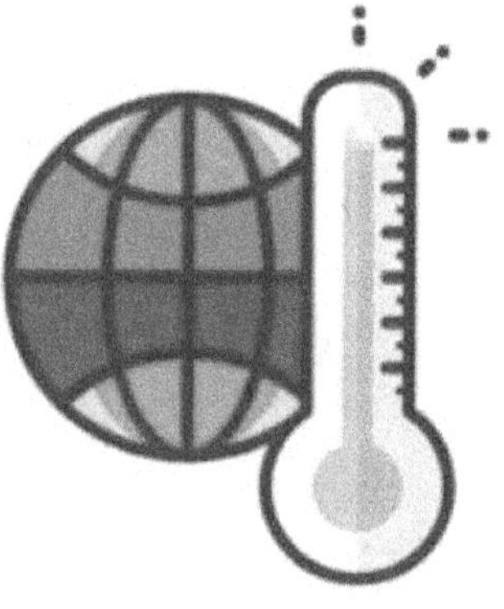

The whole world is warm today!

venteux

szeles

The leaves are blowing away since it's so windy!

tante

néni

My aunt is very nice to me.

frère

fiú testvér

My brother is very fun to play with.

cousin

unokatestvér

I love going to the playground with my cousin.

fille

lánya

I like to read books with my daughter.

père

apa

My father is playing with me.

petite fille

lány unoka

My granddaughter has blond hair.

grand-mère

nagymama

My grandmother is very old and has glasses.

petit fils

unokája

My grandson and I are very excited today!

mère

anya

My mother likes to pick me up.

neveu

unokaöcs

My father's nephew is my cousin.

nièce

unokahúg

My niece is very good at playing ball.

sœur

lánytestvér

My sister is so pretty!

fils

fiú

My son likes to play with toy cars.

belle fille

mostohalány

My stepdaughter likes the color orange.

belle-mère

mostohaanya

My stepmother is pretty.

beau-fils

mostohafiú

This is my stepson, Greg.

oncle

nagybácsi

My uncle tells lots of funny jokes.

bol

tál

The bowl has nothing inside.

tasse

csésze

My mom drinks her coffee out of a cup.

plat

tál

That dish has a bone inside.

fourchette

villa

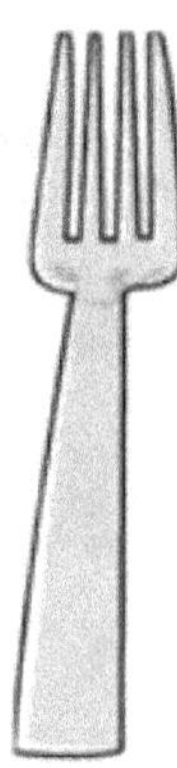

We have more spoons than forks.

verre

üveg

I have a glass of water on my desk.

couteau

kés

I have a knife in my kitchen.

agresser

bögre

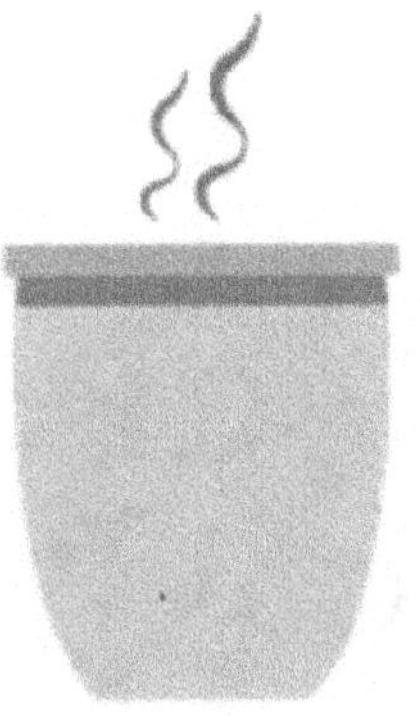

This mug of coffee is for my dad.

serviette de table

szalvéta

You can use the napkins to clean your hands.

poivre

bors

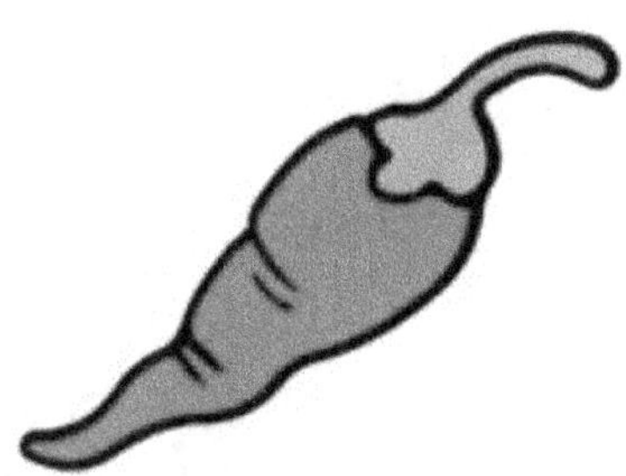

The pepper is very spicy.

lanceur

kancsó

Pour yourself some lemonade from the pitcher.

assiette

lemez

Can you help me wash the plates?

salade

saláta

The salad is very healthy for you.

sel

só

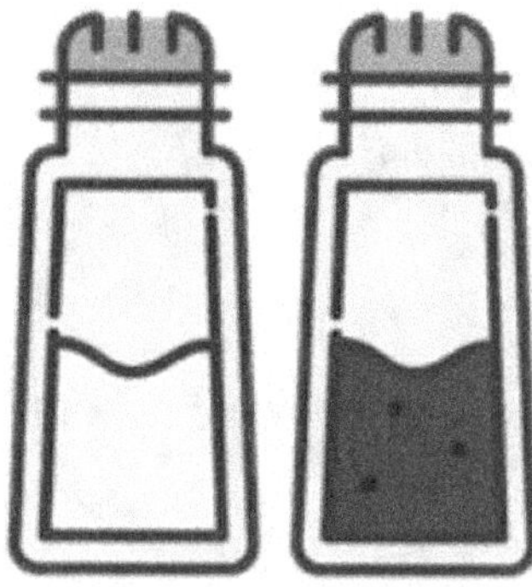

The salt tastes good with a few pinches of pepper.

soucoupe

csészealj

The plate is for my cup.

cuillère

kanál

I use a spoon to eat my rice.

sucre

cukor

The pack of sugar is very heavy.

dimanche

vasárnap

Sunday

Sunday is the day to go to Church!

lundi

hétfő

Monday

Monday is the day to start school.

mardi

kedd

Tuesday

We will go to the shops on Tuesday.

mercredi

szerda

Wednesday

Wednesday is hard to spell!

jeudi

csütörtök

Thursday

Thursday is the fourth day of the week!

vendredi

péntek

Friday

My birthday is on Friday!

samedi

szombat

Saturday

Saturday is the weekend!

cuire

süt

The chef will bake a cake.

ébullition

forral

I will boil the eggs.

griller

civakodás

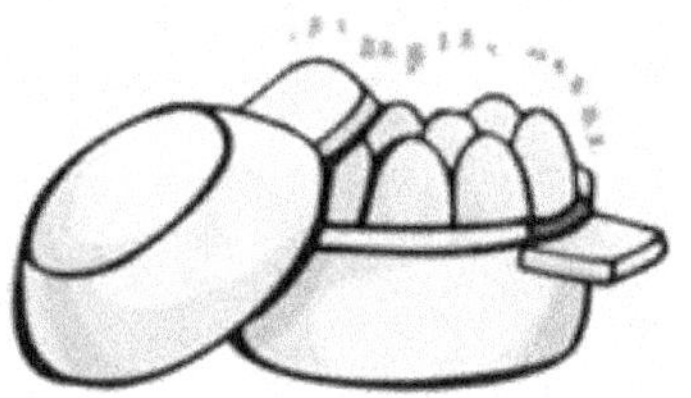

Broil is very yummy.

ouvre-boîte

konzervnyitó

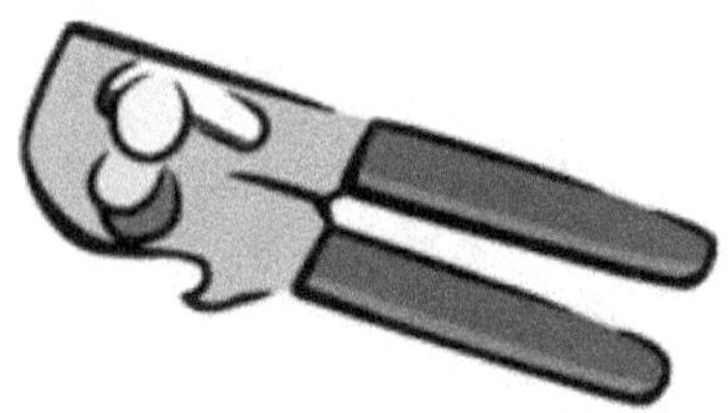

That can opener is used for opening cans.

frire

süt

The pan can fry lots of things.

gril

rostély

We have a grill in our backyard.

tasse à mesurer

mérőedény

My mom uses the measuring cup for baking.

cuillère à mesurer

mérőkanál

I use a measuring spoon to eat my dessert.

four micro onde

mikrohullámú sütő

The microwave is used to heat food.

bol à mélanger

keverő tál

She is using the mixing bowl to mix things.

serviettes en papier

papírtörlő

Dry your hands with paper towels.

poché aux œufs

tojáscsőr

The poach is put on noodles.

porte pot

edényfogó

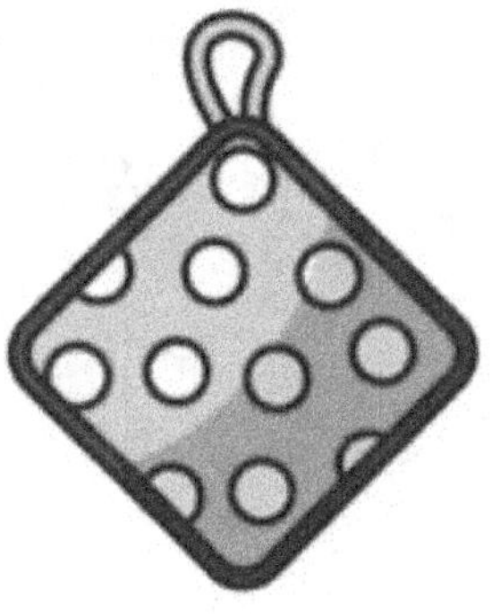

The potholder is soft.

rôti

sült

The chef made roast chicken.

rouleau à pâtisserie

sodrófa

He is holding a rolling pin.

brouiller

tülekedés

My mom is making scrambled eggs for breakfast.

mijoter

lassú tűzön süt

The simmer is rice today.

couteau

kés

The knife is sharp.

cuillère

kanál

I eat my food with a spoon and fork.

spatule

spatula

The spatula will help us flip the steak over.

vapeur

gőz

The steam is coming from the pot.

passoire

szűrő

The strainer is used to strain stuff.

minuteur

időzítő

I set my timer for 12:00.

fourchette

villa

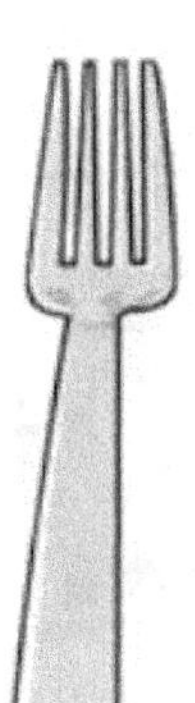

I have lots of metallic forks.

grille-pain

kenyérpirító

The toaster will toast my bread.

bouilloire

vízforraló

The kettle has tea inside.

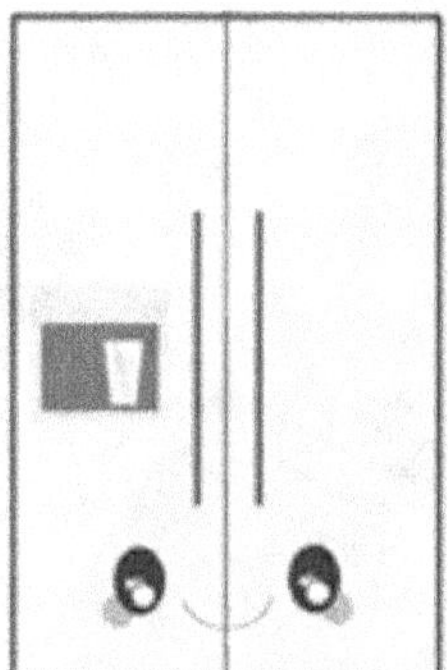

réfrigérateur

hűtőszekrény

The refrigerator has lots of things inside.

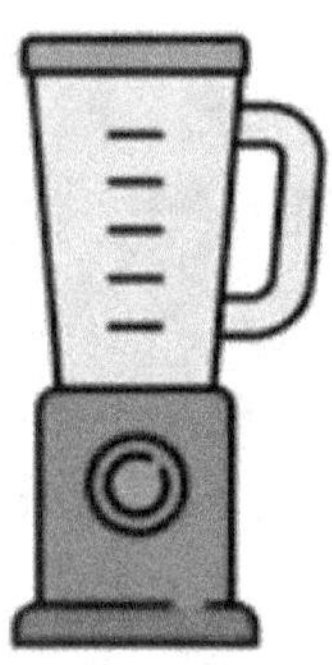

mixeur

turmixgép

The blender will mix up my fruits.

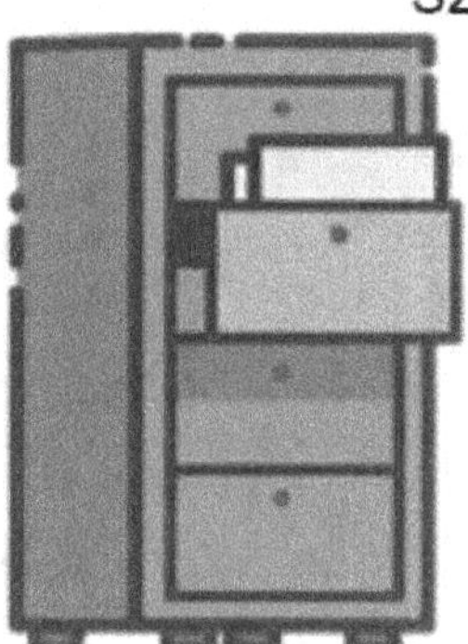

cabinets

szekrények

The cabinet has my paper inside.

placard

szekrény

The cupboard has lots of books.

four micro onde

mikrohullámú sütő

The microwave will heat my food.

arrière

vissza

She has a slender back.

des joues

arcon

She kisses her mom on the cheek.

poitrine

mellkas

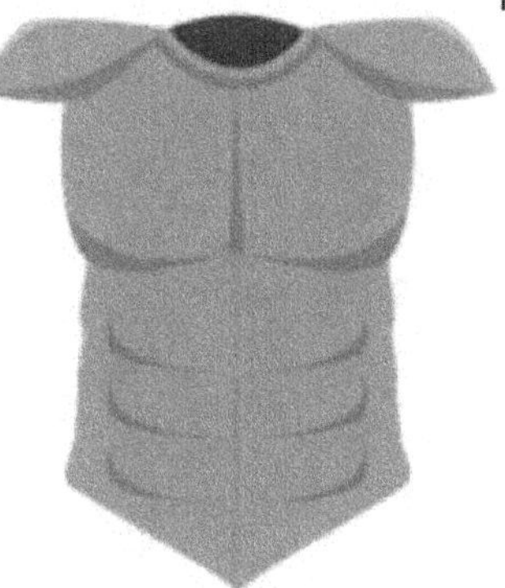

The armor is for your chest.

menton

áll

This is my chin!

oreilles

fülek

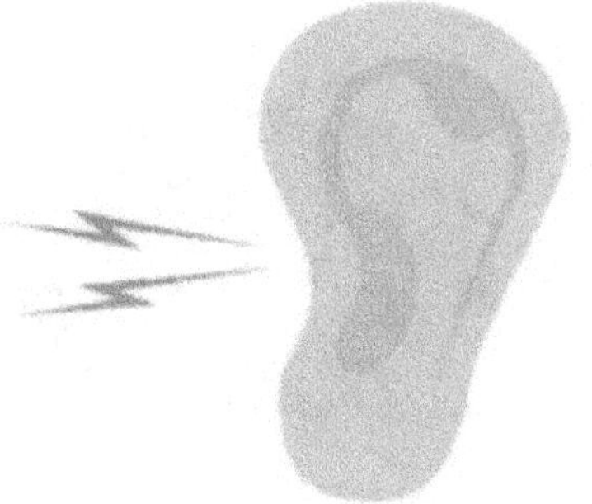

The ear is hearing something.

les sourcils

szemöldök

The eyebrows are raised.

yeux

szemek

The eyes are blue.

pieds

láb

I have one pair of feet.

des doigts

ujjak

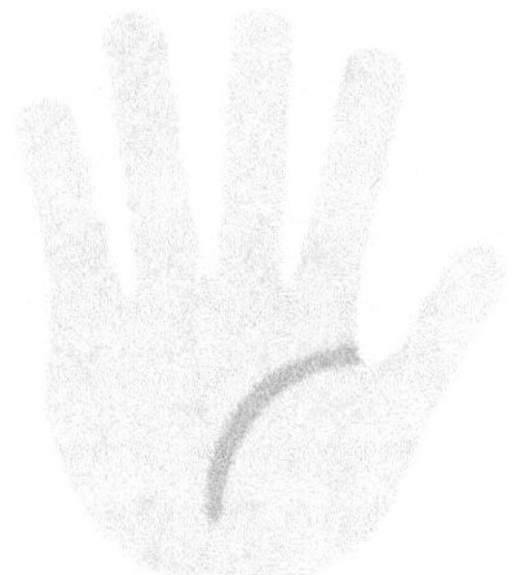

The fingers are waving at us.

pied

láb

My foot has five fingers.

front

homlok

My brain is behind my forehead.

cheveux

haj

My hair is long and black.

mains

kezek

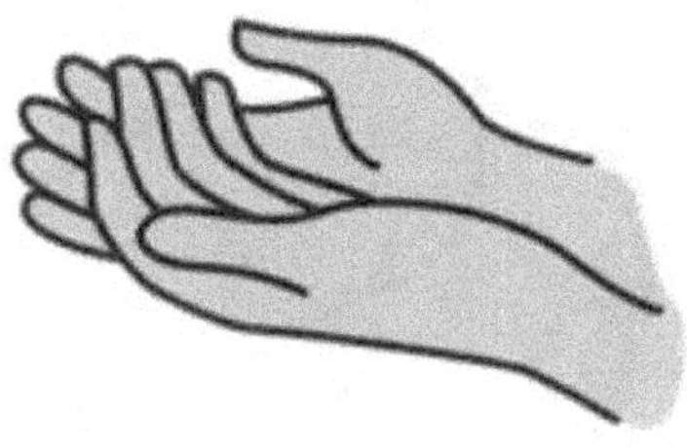

I will wash my hands in the sink.

tête

fej

She has a big head.

les hanches

csípő

The gorilla has his hands on his hips.

les genoux

térd

She is begging on her knees.

jambes

lábak

The tiger has strong legs.

lèvres

ajkak

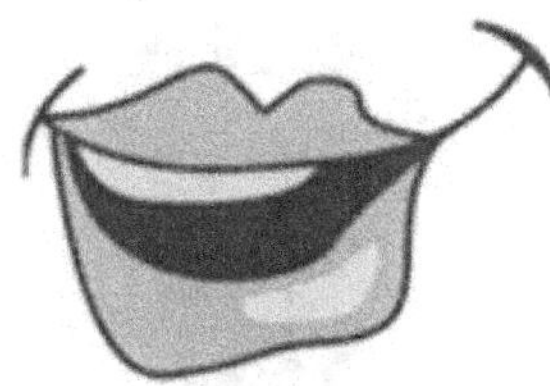

The lips have lipstick on.

bouche

száj

He is covering his mouth with his hand.

cou

nyak

The necklace is very special to me.

nez

orr

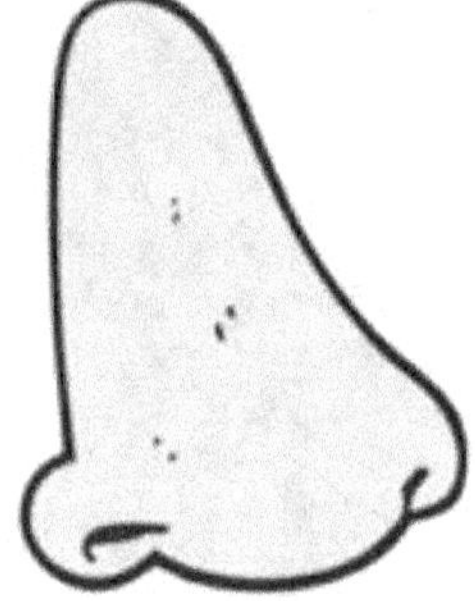

The nose smells something.

épaules

vállak

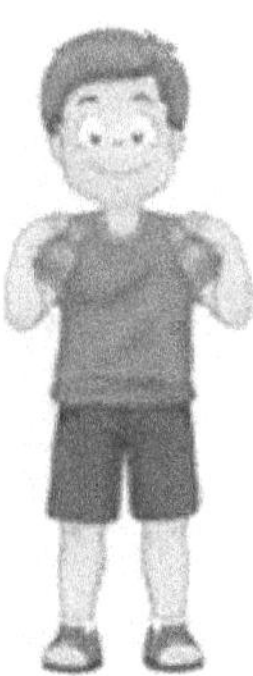

He puts his hands on his shoulders.

estomac

gyomor

He has a big stomach.

les dents

fogak

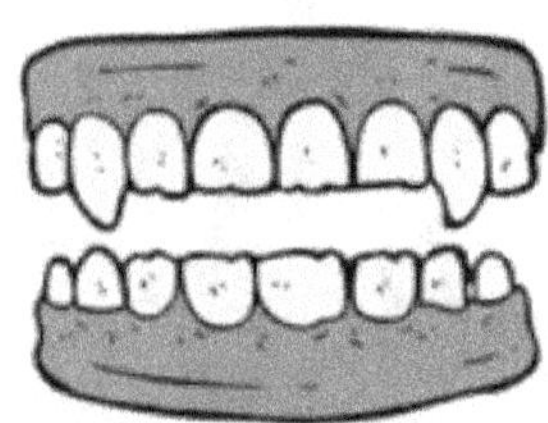

The teeth are clean and white.

gorge

torok

He has a sore throat today.

les orteils

lábujjak

My toes are small.

langue

nyelv

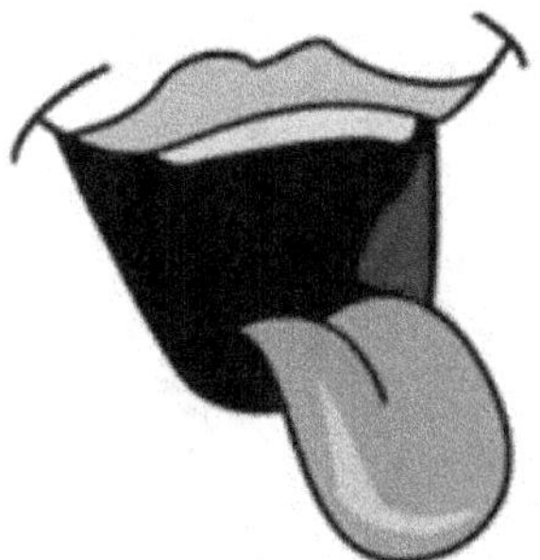

My tongue is licking ice cream.

dent

fog

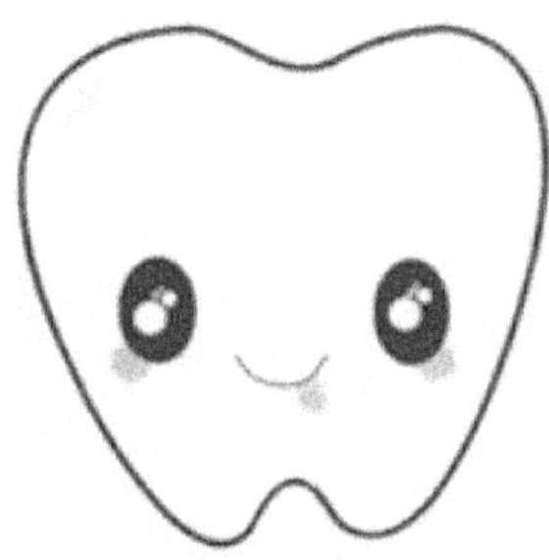

The tooth has big eyes.

taille

derék

He has his hands on his waist.

salopette

overall

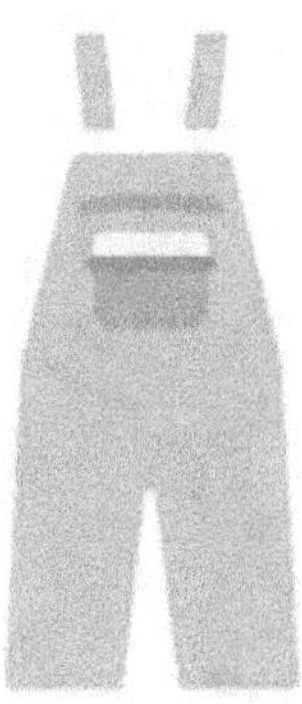

I bought these overalls for you!

mitaines

ujjatlan kesztyű

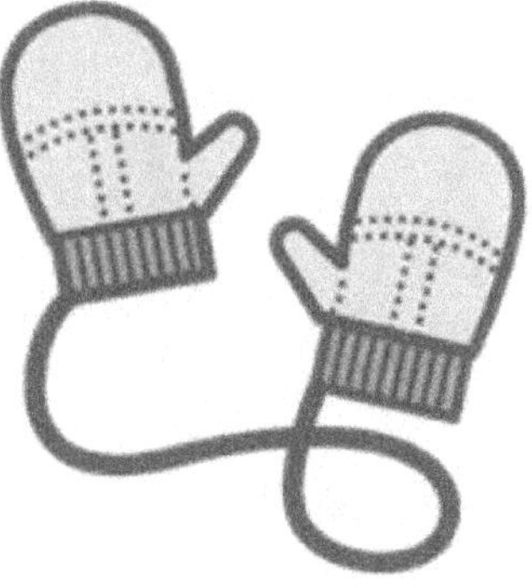

The mittens are very warm.

bonnet

kötött sapka

The beanie is for winter.

tablier

kötény

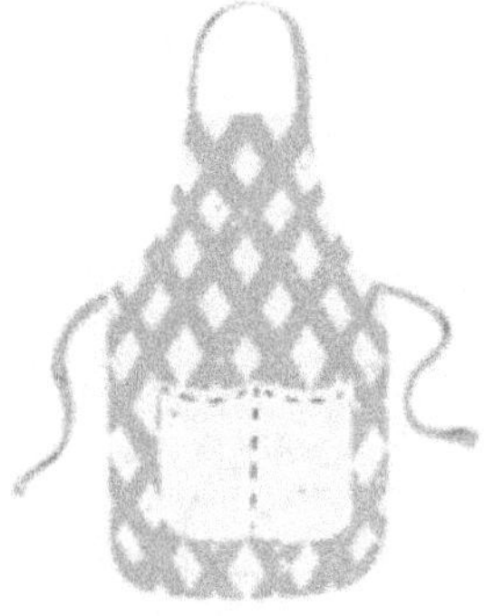

I wear my apron when I bake.

poupée

baba

The doll is for my baby sister.

hochets

csörgő

The rattle is for the baby.

jouet

játék

The toy is very fun.

couche

pelenka

The baby has to wear a diaper.

berceau

mózeskosár

She is sleeping in her bassinet.

bavoir

iddogál

My baby brother has to wear his
bib when he is eating.

octogone

nyolcszög

The octagon is saying okay!

triangle

háromszög

The triangle has three corners.

carré

négyzet

Square

The square has four sides.

cercle

kör

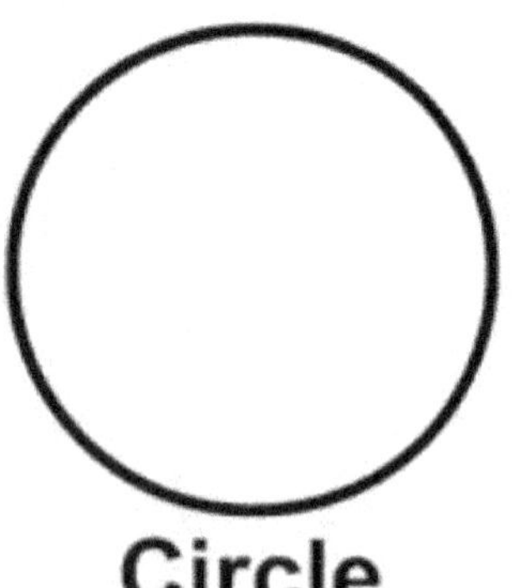

Circle

The circle is round.

ovale

ovális

The oval shape looks like a circle.

cœur

szív

I drew a heart on my paper.

traverser

kereszt

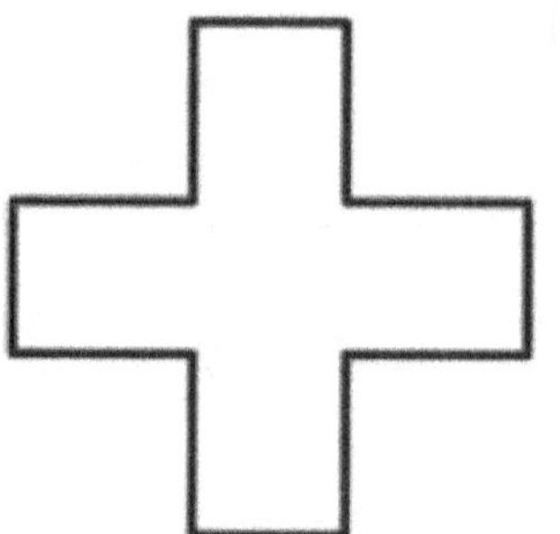

That sign is a cross.

la flèche

nyíl

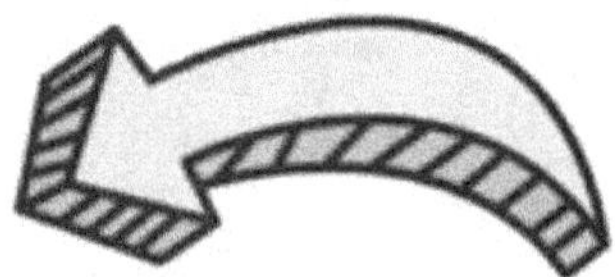

The arrow is pointing this way.

cube

kocka

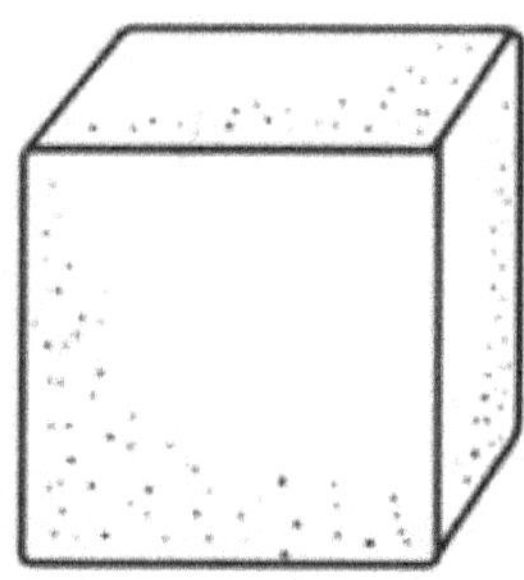

The cube is 3D.

étoile

csillag

The star is yellow and shiny.

tir à l'arc

íjászat

The archery is where you aim.

badminton

tollaslabda

My favorite sport is badminton.

criquet

krikett

I am very good at cricket.

bowling

bowling

I got one pin down at bowling!

boxe

dobozolás

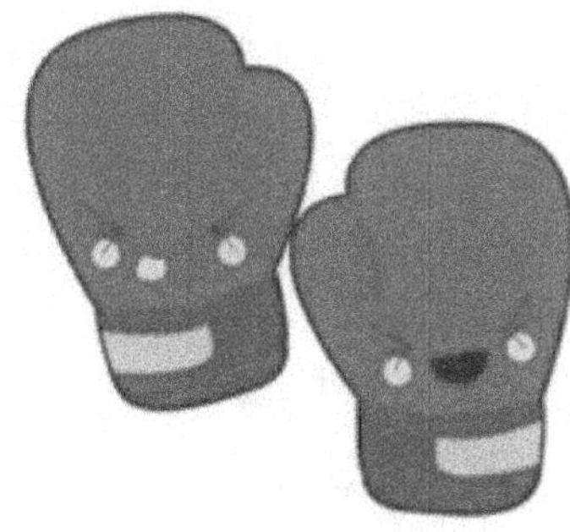

The boxing gloves are hot.

tennis

tenisz

He can hit the ball in tennis.

faire de la planche a roulettes

gördeszkázás

He skateboards to school.

planche de surf

szörfözni

The shark loves surfing in the ocean.

le hockey

jégkorong

I like to play Ice hockey.

yoga

jóga

He is closing his eyes and doing yoga.

épée

swordplay

They are fencing and dueling together.

aptitude

alkalmasság

She will do some fitness in the pool.

gymnastique

gimnasztika

He can do brilliant gymnastics.

karaté

karate

She is good at kicking in Karate.

volley-ball

röplabda

She is holding a volleyball.

musculation

súlyemelés

The girl with brown hair can do weightlifting.

basketball

kosárlabda

He can balance the ball with one finger in basketball.

base-ball

baseball

The little chick is in the finales at baseball.

le rugby

rögbi

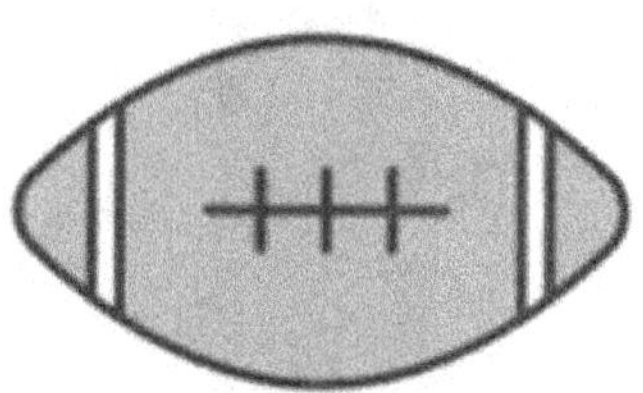

The rugby ball has white stripes.

lutte

birkózás

The sumo will compete in wrestling.

course de voitures

autóverseny

He is number one for car racing.

cyclisme

kerékpározás

He is peacefully cycling on the road.

fonctionnement

futás

He is running while listening to his earphones.

tennis de table

asztali tenisz

My brother and dad will play table tennis.

pêche

halászat

He will go to the river to fish.

judo

cselgáncs

She has a red belt in Judo.

escalade

mászó

He will climb the ladder.

tournage

lövés

He is shooting the archery board.

le golf

golf

She is going to compete in the golf competition.

balade

lovagol

He will ride his scooter.

asseyez-vous

ülj le

They are sitting down together.

se lever

állj fel

She likes to stand up.

bats toi

harc

They are fighting over the book.

rire

nevetés

He is laughing so hard!

lis

olvas

She read a picture book.

jouer

játék

He went to play on the slide.

ecoutez

hallgat

He listened for the ice cream cart.

pleurer

kiáltás

He cried because he got a bad grade.

pense

gondol

He thought that the test would be hard.

chanter

énekel

He sang for the concert.

regarder la télévision

tv-t néz

He watched TV the whole night.

danse

tánc

She was a good dancer.

allumer

bekapcsol

The light is turned on.

éteindre

kikapcsolni

The light is turned off.

gagner

győzelem

He won the contest.

mouche

légy

The parrot can fly.

couper

vágott

He was cutting his nails.

désinvolte

dobd el

He threw away the garbage.

dormir

alvás

He slept soundly.

fermer

bezárás

He closed his mouth shut.

ouvert

nyisd ki

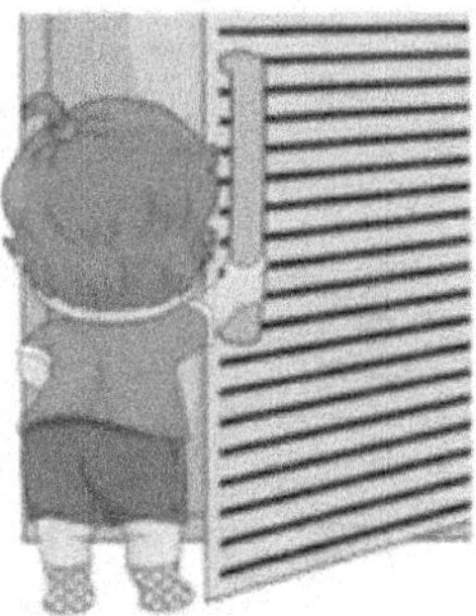

She opened the bathroom door.

écrire

ír

She wrote with a pencil.

donner

adni

Santa gave her a present.

sauter

ugrás

She had fun jumping.

manger

eszik

The shark ate yummy ice cream.

boisson

ital

The old British man drank tea.

cuisinier

szakács

The microwave cooked his soup.

lavage

mosás

You need to remember to wash your hands.

attendre

várjon

He was waiting for the bus.

montée

mászik

She climbed a lot of mountains.

parler

beszélgetés

Two best friends were talking together.

crawl

csúszik

The baby crawled on the floor.

rêver

álom

The Sloth dreamed about eating leaves.

creuser

ás

That strong man dug a swimming pool.

taper

taps

The baby clapped her hands.

tricoter

kötött

She knits with the purple string.

coudre

varr

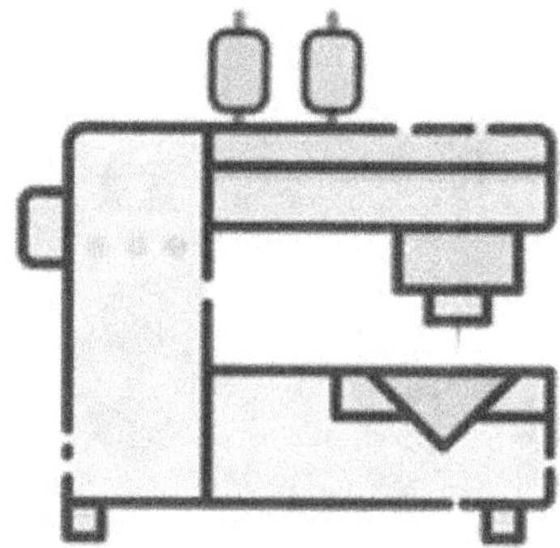

That is a sewing machine.

odeur

szag

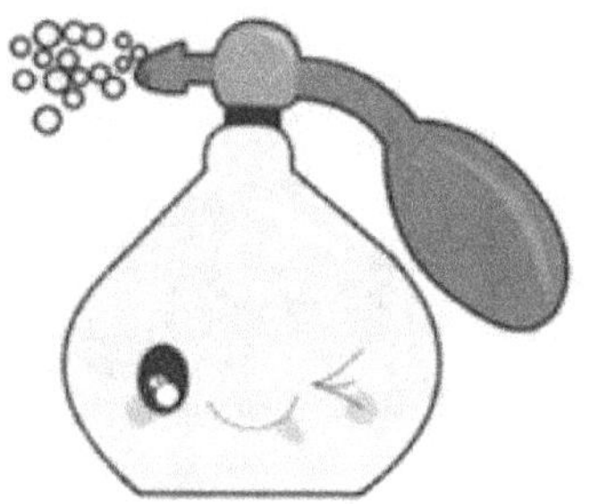

The perfume smelled great.

baiser

csók

He kissed his mother.

étreinte

ölelés

They hugged each other.

ronfler

horkolás

The tiger snored.

baigner

fürdik

He took a bath.

s'incliner

meghajolva

He bowed to the judge.

peindre

festék

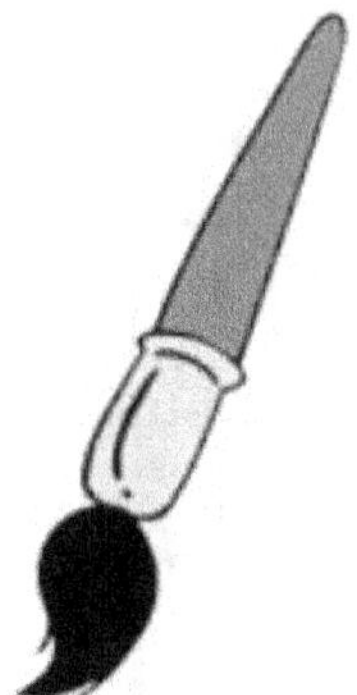

He painted a colorful picture.

se plonger

zuhanás

He dove to the deepest part of the ocean.

ski

sí

The ski was expensive.

empiler

kazal

The books are stacked high.

acheter

megvesz

They bought cereal.

secouer

ráz

They shook hands together.

programmeur

programozó

He was a smart computer programmer.

vétérinaire

állatorvos

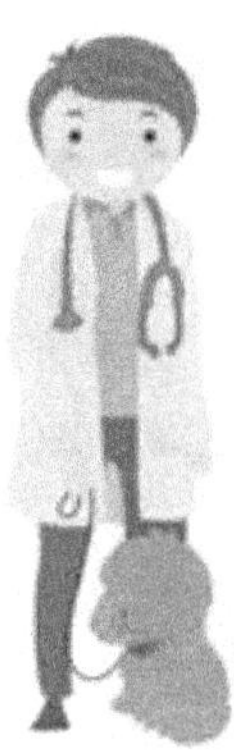

She is a veterinarian.

vendeur de rue

utcai árus

That street vendor sells hot dogs.

mineur

bányász

That Miner will find gold.

prof

tanár

The owl is the teacher.

groom

londiner

That Bellboy is fat.

orateur

hangszóró

The chicken is a great Speaker.

boucher

hentes

The Butcher sells fish.

pharmacien

gyógyszerész

That Pharmacist saved a person's life.

réceptionniste

recepciós

He is a Receptionist.

politicien

politikus

He wants to be a Politician.

guide touristique

idegenvezető

That Tour guide led us around Japan.

entrepreneur

vállalkozó

He is an Entrepreneur.

danseuse de ballet

balett táncos

She is training to be a Ballet dancer.

astronaute

űrhajós

He is a great astronaut.

juge

bíró

That Judge is always fair.

The lawyer is serious.

She is a cashier at the market.

He is a fast Taxi driver.

That Plumber fixes toilets.

She wants to be a Musician like her teacher.

The chef makes fast food.

boulanger

pék

That baker is a bread.

artiste

művész

That Artist came from Italy.

acteur

színész

That actor is famous.

barman

kocsmáros

The Bartender works in a bar.

coiffeur

fodrász

That girl is a Hairdresser.

évêques

püspöki

He is a Bishop.

opticien

látszerész

She went to an Optician.

fleuriste

virágárus

She is a great Florist.

écrivain

író

He is a famous author.

comptable

könyvelő

My accountant is loyal.

du vin

bor

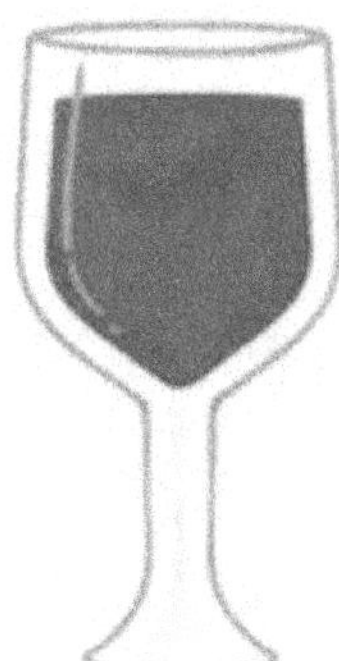

That wine tastes good.

café

kávé

That coffee is bitter.

limonade

limonádé

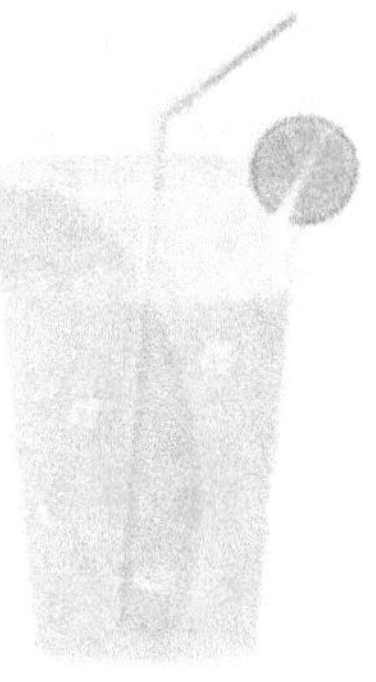

The lemonade is refreshing.

chocolat chaud

forró csokoládé

I drink hot chocolate every day.

milk-shake

milkshake

The milkshake has whipped cream.

eau

víz

The water is not cold.

thé

tea

The tea is hot.

lait

tej

Milk is white.

bière

sör

The beer is foamy.

un soda

szóda

The soda is fizzy.

smoothie

turmix

The smoothie is a watermelon flavor.

milk-shake

milkshake

The milkshake has whipped cream.

lait de coco

kókusztej

The coconut milk is yummy.

du jus d'orange

narancslé

The orange juice is made from oranges.

cacao

kakaó

The cocoa is sweet.

fromage

sajt

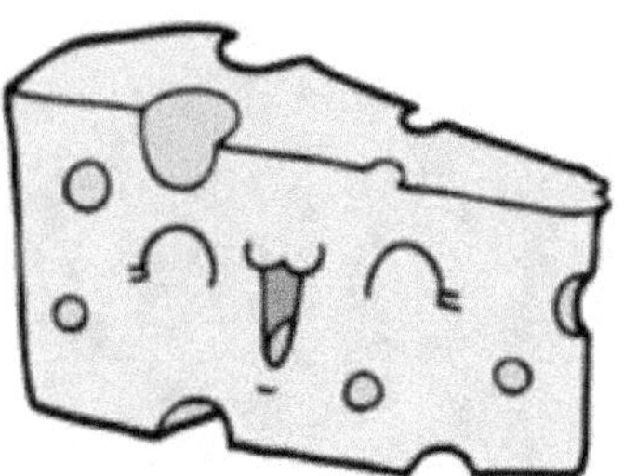

The cheese is creamy.

oeuf

tojás

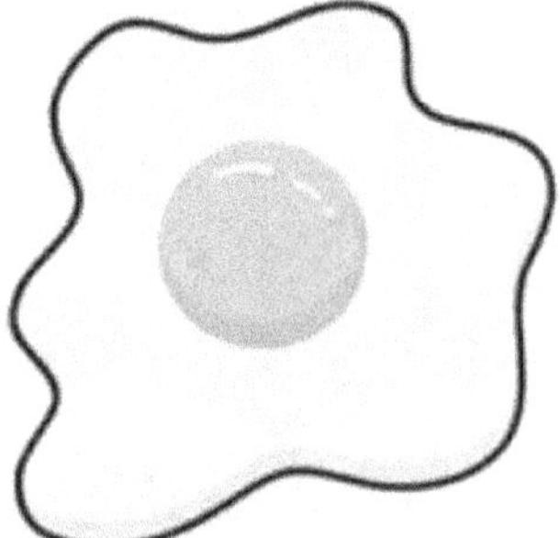

The egg is fried.

beurre

vaj

The butter is put on bread.

margarine

margarin

Margarine looks like butter.

yaourt

joghurt

That yogurt is popular.

cottage cheese

túró

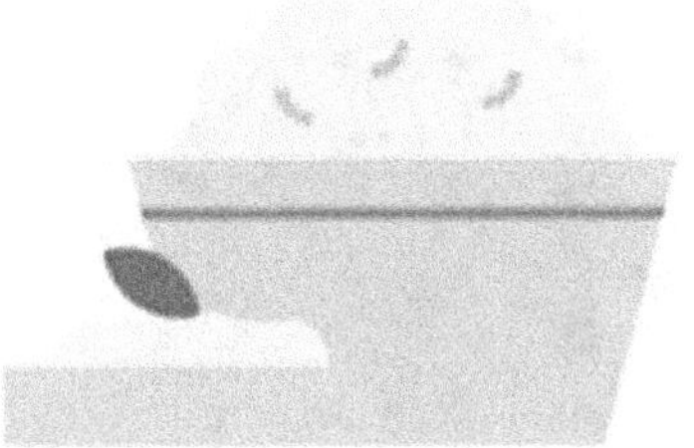

The cottage cheese is put on crackers.

crème glacée

jégkrém

They have a triple scoop ice cream.

crème

krém

That is a lot of creams.

sandwich

szendvics

That sandwich is healthy.

saucisse

kolbász

Americans love sausages.

hamburger

hamburger

That hamburger looks happy.

hot-dog

hot dog

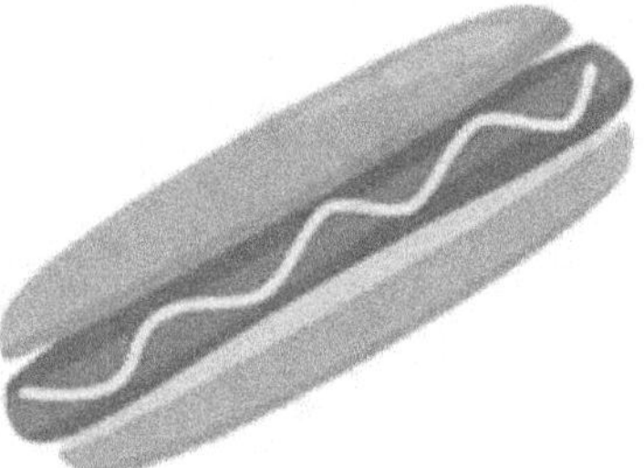

That hot dog has mustard on it.

pain

kenyér

That bread is saying hello.

pizza

pizza

That pizza is cheesy.

steak

steak

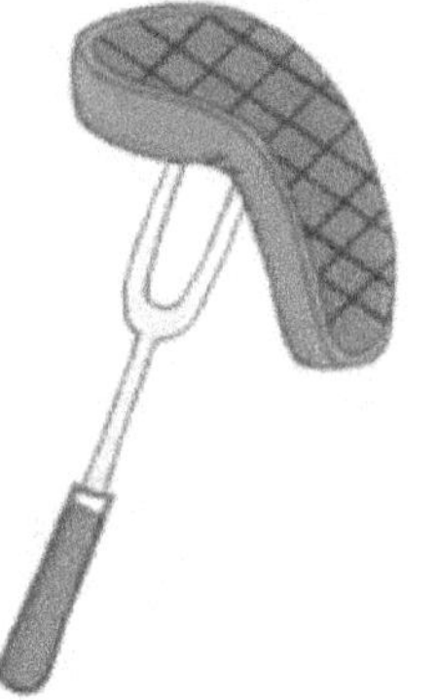

The steak was grilled.

poulet rôti

sült csirke

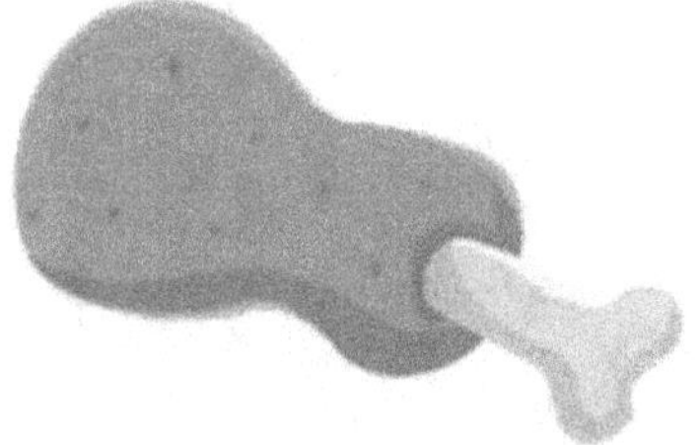

Roast Chicken is delicious.

poisson

hal

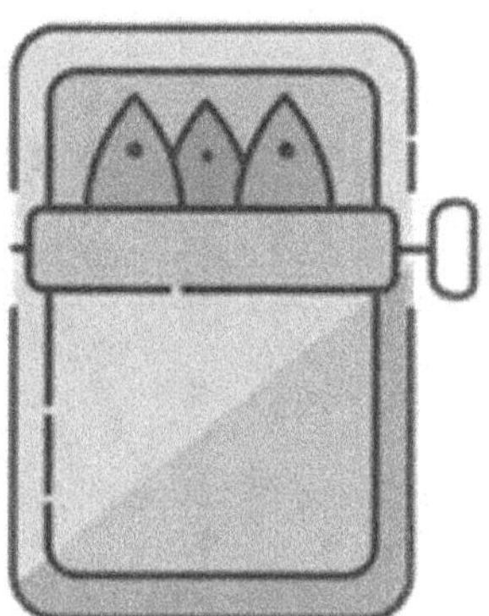

You can buy canned fish in the market.

fruit de mer

tenger gyümölcsei

Lobster is expensive seafood.

jambon

sonka

Ham can be put in sandwiches.

kebab

kebab

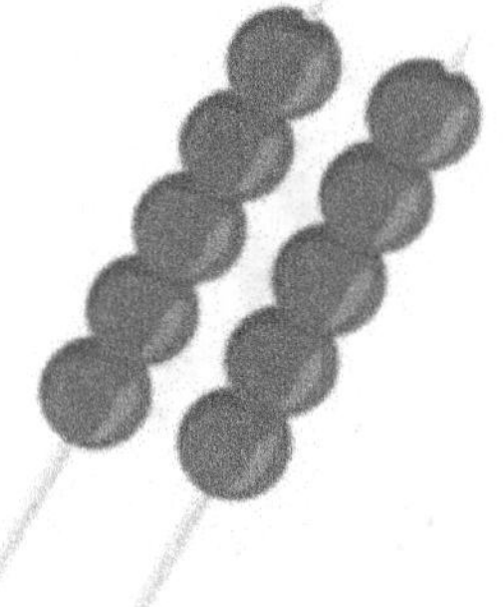

Kebab is a delicacy in America.

bacon

szalonna

That bacon is smiling.

crème fraîche

tejföl

You can dip your chips in sour cream.

vache

tehén

Cows are black and white.

lapin

nyúl

That rabbit is fun to play with.

canard

kacsa

That duck is content.

crevette

garnélarák

The shrimp has six legs.

porc

malac

That pig is pink and fat.

abeille

méh

The bee has a stinger.

chèvre

kecske

That goat has a white horn.

crabe

rák

The crab has two big pincers.

cerf

szarvas

That deer is sleeping.

dinde

pulyka

The turkey has a giant tail.

colombe

galamb

That dove is carrying a plant.

mouton

juh

That sheep has fluffy wool.

poisson

hal

That fish has colorful fins.

poulet

csirke

That chicken is waking everybody up.

cheval

ló

The horse has a red mane.

chaise

szék

That wing chair is yellow.

meuble tv

tv állvány

The TV stand can hold books.

canapé

kanapé

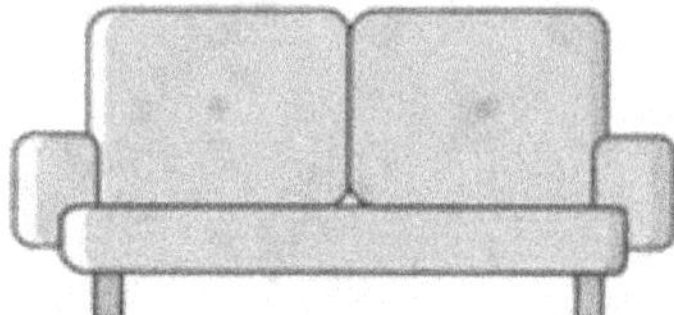

The sofa is comfortable to sit on.

coussins

ülőpárnák

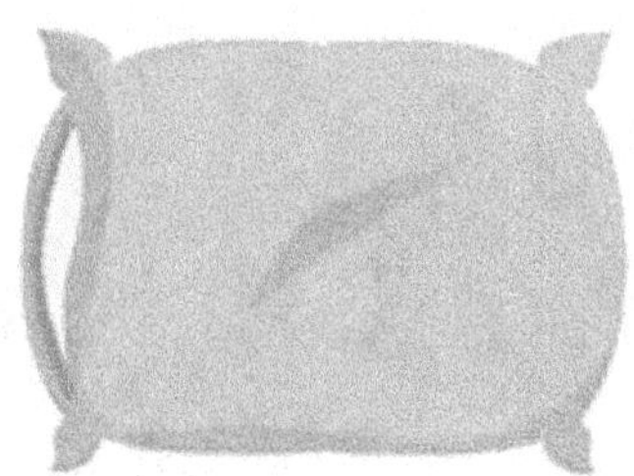

The cushion helps soften your seat.

téléphone

telefon

The telephone is ringing.

télévision

televízió

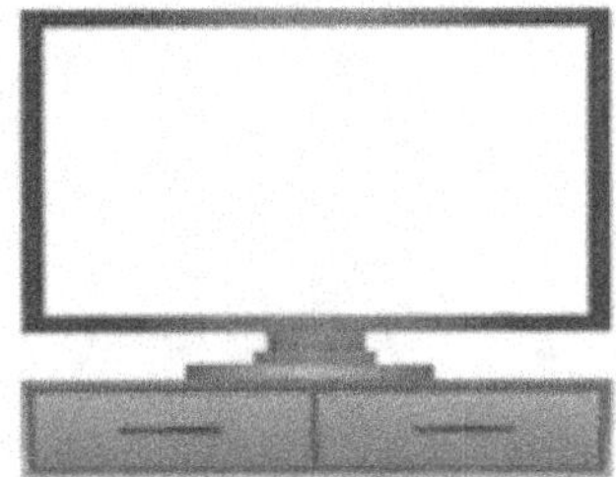

That television is big.

haut-parleurs

hangszórók

That speaker is used to increase the volume.

table d'appoint

kisasztal

That end table is sparkling clean.

service à thé

teáskészlet

That tea set is from China.

cheminée

kandalló

The fireplace makes me warm.

télécommandes

távirányítók

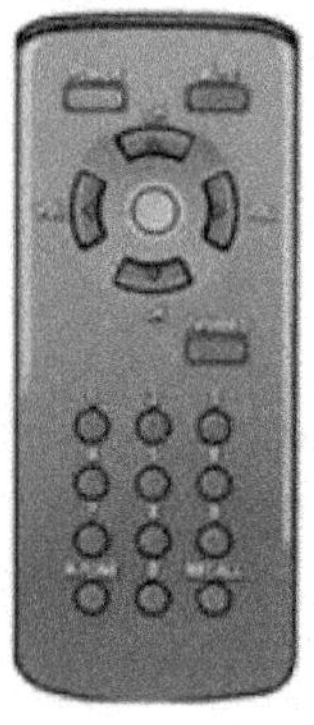

The remote has lots of buttons.

ventilateur électrique

ventillátor

The fan is blowing wind.

lampadaire

állólámpa

The floor lamp is very tall.

tapis

szőnyeg

The carpet is soft and silky.

bureaux

asztalok

The table is made of wood.

stores

vakok

I will pull the blinds down.

rideaux

függöny

She opened the curtains.

image

kép

The picture is about the mountains and the sky.

vase

váza

The roses are all in a vase.

l'horloge

óra

The alarm clock is beeping.

oreiller

párna

The pillow is pink and yellow.

cintre

kalap fogas

The hat stand has only one hat on it.

mettre la table

asztalt terít

I have made up on my dressing table.

lampe de table

asztali lámpa

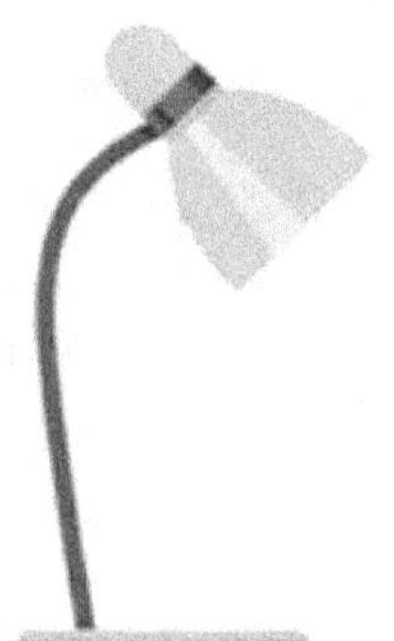

The table lamp will help me see in the dark.

miroir

tükör

The mirror is very tall.

planche a repasser

vasalódeszka

Don't touch the ironing board, it's hot!

boîte avec tiroir

doboz fiókkal

You can keep your clothes in the hope chest.

table de chevet

éjjeliszekrény

The nightstand has my lamp on it.

lit

ágy

The bed is charming.

climatisation

légkondícionáló

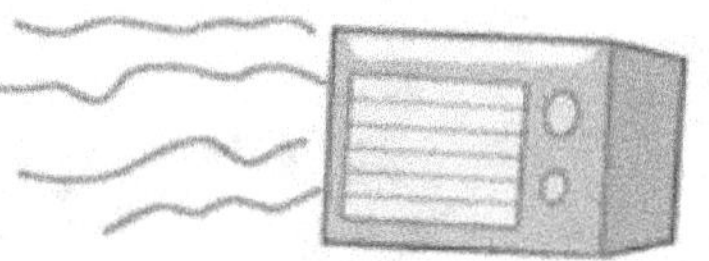

The air conditioner is cold.

cruche

kancsó

The measuring jug has nothing inside.

dentifrice

fogkrém

The toothpaste is mint flavored.

brosse à dents

fogkefe

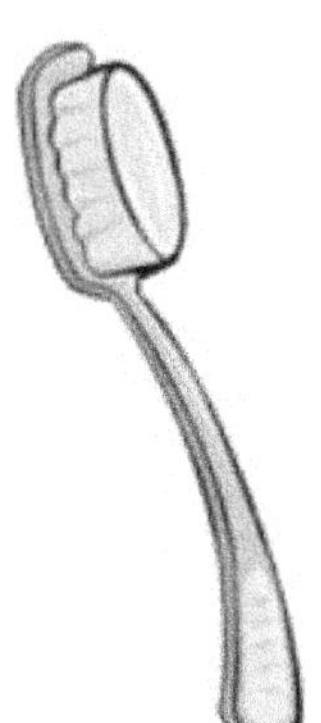

The toothbrush has toothpaste on it.

savon

szappan

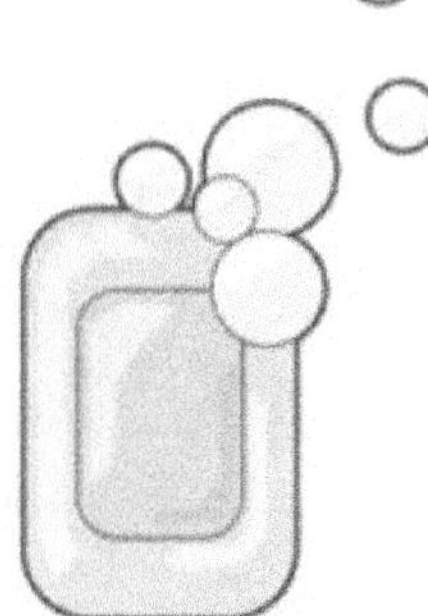

The soap is very bubbly.

pince à linge

ruhacsipesz

The clothespin will clip my clothes.

cintre

akasztó

The hanger is hanging my boots.

sèche-cheveux

hajszárító

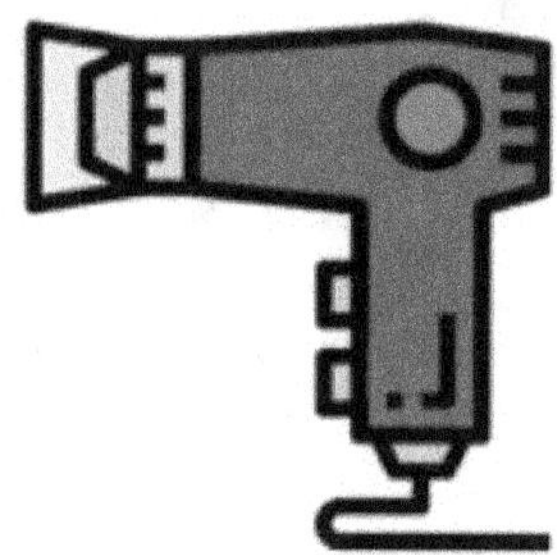

The hairdryer will blow my hair.

shampooing

sampon

The shampoo is used to clean your hair.

bulle

buborék

The bubbles are very fun to play in.

brosse

kefe

She is brushing her hair with the brush.

papier toilette

vécé papír

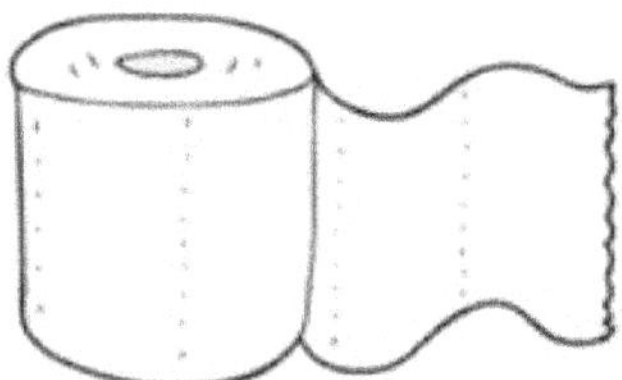

The toilet paper is used to dry your hands.

serviette

törülköző

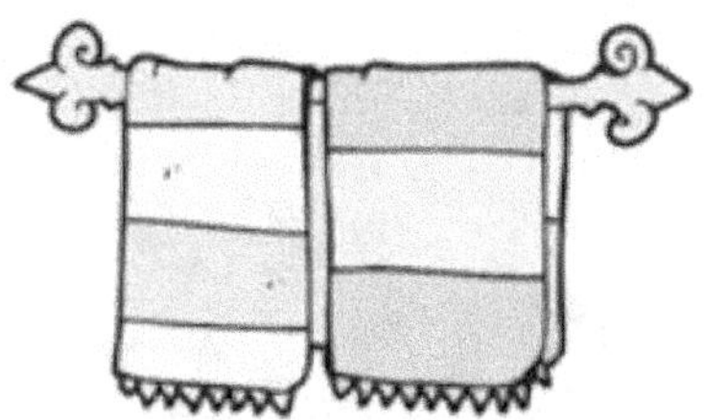

We have two towels on the rack.

corde à linge

szárítókötél

My shirt is hanging on the clothesline.

douche

zuhany

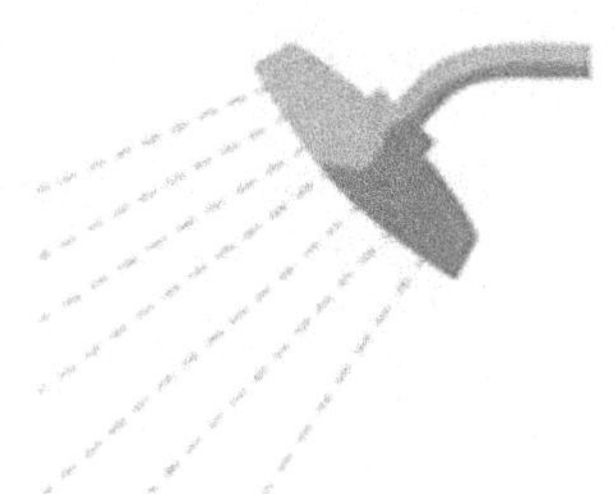

The shower is spraying water.

baignoire

fürdőkád

The bathtub is comfortable.

lessive

mosószer

The laundry detergent is used with the washing machine.

seau

vödör

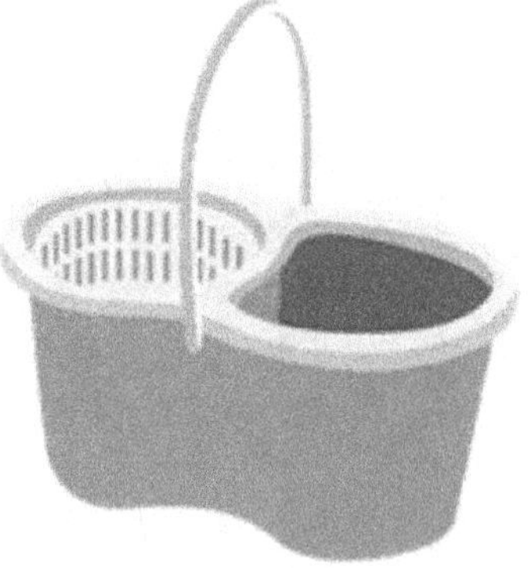

Can you help me fill up the bucket?

vadrouilles

mops

The mop is used for mopping the floor.

savon liquide

folyékony szappan

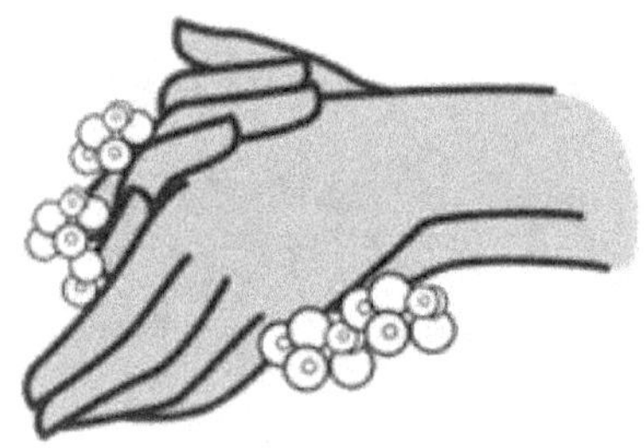

I use soapy water to wash my hands.

lessive en poudre

mosópor

I will scoop up the washing powder.

sac poubelle

szemetes zsák

The trash bag is full of trash.

poubelle

kuka

You have only to put recylcle trash in the trash can.

les puits

mosogatók

You should wash your hands in the sink.

cuvette des toilettes

wc csésze

She let her bunny use the toilet.

machine à laver

mosógép

The washing machine wash your clothes.

panier à linge

szennyes kosár

She is putting all the clothes into the laundry basket.

le rasoir

borotva

He uses the razor to shave his beard.

rasoir électrique

elektromos borotva

The electric razor works faster than the normal one.

crème à raser

borotvahab

The shaving cream is fluffy.

bain de bouche

szájvíz

The mouthwash smells very lovely.

coton-tige

pamut rügy

Q-tip can be used for many things.

brosse à cheveux

hajkefe

She brushes her hair with her hairbrush.

peigne

fésű

Her dad will comb her hair for her.

nettoyant

tisztító

Put the cap back on the cleanser bottle.

échelle

skála

You can measure things on the scale.

papier de soie

papír zsebkendő

The tissue is on the counter.

jouets de bain

fürdőjátékok

The little duck is a bath toy.

robinet

csap

The faucet is broken.

miroir

tükör

He is looking in the mirror.

tapis de bain

fürdőszoba szőnyeg

The bath mat is purple and yellow.